D0459044

COMING UP CLUTCH

THE GREATEST UPSETS, COMEBACKS, AND FINISHES IN SPORTS HISTORY

Matt Doeden

MILLBROOK PRESS · MINNEAPOLIS

Copyright © 2019 by Lerner Publishing Group, Inc.

All rights reserved. International copyright secured. No part of this book may be reproduced, stored in a retrieval system, or transmitted in any form or by any means—electronic, mechanical, photocopying, recording, or otherwise—without the prior written permission of Lerner Publishing Group, Inc., except for the inclusion of brief quotations in an acknowledged review.

Millbrook Press
A division of Lerner Publishing Group, Inc.
241 First Avenue North
Minneapolis, MN 55401 USA

For reading levels and more information, look up this title at www.lernerbooks.com.

Main body text set in Adobe Garamond Pro Regular 14/19.
Typeface provided by Adobe Systems.

Library of Congress Cataloging-in-Publication Data

Names: Doeden, Matt, author.
Title: Coming up clutch : the greatest upsets, comebacks, and finishes in sports history / Matt Doeden.
Description: Minneapolis : Millbrook Press, [2019] | Audience: Age 10–18. | Audience: Grade 9 to 12. | Includes bibliographical references and index.
Identifiers: LCCN 2017047697 (print) | LCCN 2018000926 (ebook) | ISBN 9781541524750 (eb pdf) | ISBN 9781512427561 (lb : alk. paper)
Subjects: LCSH: Sports—United States—History—Anecdotes—Juvenile literature. | Sports upsets—Juvenile literature. | Comebacks—Juvenile literature.
Classification: LCC GV583 (ebook) | LCC GV583 .D64 2019 (print) | DDC 796.0973—dc23

LC record available at https://lccn.loc.gov/2017047697

Manufactured in the United States of America
1-41491-23352-2/22/2018

CONTENTS

INTRODUCTION:
WHAT IS CLUTCH?

Clutch. It's a term that's often used in sports. We reserve it for players or teams who come up big when the stakes are highest. It's an extra-inning home run, a Super Bowl–winning touchdown pass, or a last-second shot that changes a game. Coming up clutch is what separates the merely good from the legendary.

Yet as often as fans use the term *clutch*, it remains something of a mystery. What makes one athlete a clutch player while another chokes in high-pressure situations? Is it better gear or mental preparation? Is it simply circumstances or just luck? Is there a clutch gene? Are there really clutch players and teams, or does it just seem that way to fans wrapped up in their favorite sports?

How does an athlete come up clutch? By overcoming the odds, no matter how long they seem. By making the perfect pass, shot, or play at just the right time. By elevating his or her performance when the pressure is on.

David Tyree of the New York Giants catches the football by pressing it against his helmet during Super Bowl XLII on February 3, 2008. *Sports Illustrated* named it the 19th greatest moment in sports history.

Man o' War (*right*) entered 21 races in his career and won all but one of them.

1 BUCKING THE ODDS:

THE GREATEST UPSETS

There's something about an athlete or a team overcoming the greatest of odds that inspires sports fans. Many people can't help but pull for the underdog to knock off a heavy favorite. Usually, fans expect favorites to win for a reason. They have more talent, better resources, more experienced coaching—or all of those advantages. Yet sometimes, in spite of everything, underdogs come up clutch and shock the sports world. It's the art of the upset, and it's one of the most thrilling moments in sports.

UPSET
AUGUST 13, 1919

Horse racing was among the most popular sports in the United States in 1919, and no horse was more celebrated than Man o' War. The thoroughbred stood toe-to-toe with baseball's Babe Ruth as one of the most beloved sports figures. Man o' War's blend of power and grace was unmatched. He was so dominant that other horse owners avoided racing against him.

Man o' War defeated every horse he ever ran against—except one. The lone loss of his career came to a horse fittingly named Upset. It happened at the Sanford Stakes at Saratoga Race Course in New York on August 13, 1919. The race started out with controversy. The track did not have a starting gate. Instead, the horses lined up behind a starting tape. According to reports, the starting gun fired before Man o' War was ready. He got out slowly, drifting back in the field.

That opened an opportunity for the other horses. Two racers, Golden Broom and Upset, charged to the front while Man o' War had to pick his way through the field. Man o' War began to catch up and charged past Golden Broom into second place. *New York Times* reporter Fred Van Ness described the action: "Steadily Man o' War drew up on Upset. . . . [I]t became a question whether Upset could last to win."

The two horses sprinted to the finish line, with Man o' War charging ever closer to the front. He got within a neck of Upset, but the underdog surged across the line, holding a slim lead and delivering the most shocking of results.

Man o' War never lost again and became a horse-racing legend. But for some, the lingering memory of one of the greatest horses the sport has ever seen is losing to a previously unknown horse named Upset.

Man o' War (*left*) beat Upset (*right*) in six of their seven career races together.

THE MIRACLE ON ICE
FEBRUARY 22, 1980

In 1980 the United States and the Soviet Union (present-day Russia and nearby countries) stood as the world's two superpowers. However, in the realm of Olympic hockey, the Soviets stood alone. Their team was a powerhouse that had won six of the past seven gold medals at the Winter Olympics. The team was filled with proven veterans, most of whom had been playing together for years.

By contrast, the United States had never had a great national team. The 1980 US Olympic team was composed of 20 amateur players—12 of whom came from Minnesota, the home state of head coach Herb Brooks. They were the youngest team at the Winter Olympics that year and the youngest national team the United States had ever put together.

So when the two teams met in Lake Placid, New York, on February 22 for an Olympic showdown, there was little reason to believe the United States could compete. After all, the Soviets had drubbed the Americans in an earlier match that year, 10–3. A *New York Times* writer declared that the only way that the Soviet Union wouldn't beat the Americans and then go on to win the gold medal would be for the arena's ice to melt. The result of the game seemed to be such a foregone conclusion that ABC didn't even televise the match live. Viewers had to watch it on a delay.

The Soviets came out on the attack to take an early lead, but the US team, spurred on by the friendly crowd, fought back. Mark Johnson slapped one into the Soviet net with just one second remaining in the first period to tie the game, 2–2.

Soviet head coach Viktor Tikhonov was frustrated that goaltender Vladislav Tretiak had allowed two goals. Most experts considered Tretiak to be the best goalie in the international game. Yet Tikhonov made a shocking move by replacing him with backup Vladimir Myshkin after the first period.

The Soviet Union (*in red*) attacked the United States with 12 shots on goal in the second period. Team USA managed just two shots during the period.

At first, the move seemed to work out for the Soviets. They dominated the second period, adding a goal to take a 3–2 lead. That's when everything changed. About eight minutes into the third period, Johnson scored again for the United States. About two minutes later, Team USA's Mark Pavelich slid a pass to Mike Eruzione. Eruzione had just come onto the ice, and the Soviets had failed to defend him. All alone, he drew back his stick and rifled a shot past Myshkin. US fans in the arena erupted as the Americans celebrated a 4–3 lead.

Ten minutes remained in the final period. The Soviets, not used to playing from behind, launched a furious attack. As the minutes ticked away, they lost their trademark discipline. Desperate, they took every shot that came their way rather than trying to set up quality scoring chances. US goalie Jim Craig turned away every shot.

The roar of the home crowd drew to a fever pitch as the final seconds ticked away. Even TV announcer Al Michaels couldn't hide his excitement in the final seconds as he delivered one of the most iconic calls in sports history: "Do you believe in miracles? Yes!"

The players mobbed one another on the ice. The mighty Soviet Union had gone down, while the United States, the team nobody would have predicted, went on to win the gold medal. Almost four decades later, Team USA's miracle on ice remains one of the most celebrated upsets in sports history.

SWEET 16
MARCH 1998

Upsets are common in some sports. Underdog baseball teams routinely take down favorites. The history of boxing is littered with surprises. But women's college basketball is not such a sport. Traditionally, major upsets are rare, especially in the sport's biggest showcase, the NCAA Women's Basketball Tournament. The most powerful teams usually mow down lesser competition, which is a big part of the reason that a small handful of schools—Connecticut, Tennessee, and Stanford among them—have dominated the sport for decades.

The 64-team NCAA Tournament is split into four regions. The 16 teams in each region are seeded based on their records, the difficulty of their schedules, and other factors. In the first round, the top and bottom seeds in each region face off in what had always been a formality. Top-ranked teams simply do not lose in the first round to one of the weakest teams in the tournament.

So, in 1998, when Harvard, the 16th seed in the region, faced off with top-seeded Stanford, few fans expected a close game. Harvard had enjoyed an excellent season, going 22–4. However, the relative weakness of the other teams in their conference, the Ivy League, and a lack of success against highly ranked teams left them at the bottom of the tournament heap. For the third straight year, they entered the tournament as a 16th seed. Even with Stanford dealing with several injuries, the game had the look of a blowout.

"No one thought Harvard would beat Stanford," said Harvard coach Kathy Delaney-Smith. "No one thinks Harvard would beat anyone. That's not an unusual thing."

Spurred on by what Harvard felt was a lack of respect, the team came out firing. They built a 10-point lead early in the second half. Predictably, Stanford roared back to erase Harvard's lead and take a 65–62 advantage.

That's when Harvard's Allison Feaster took over. The dynamic, high-scoring guard cut to the basket for a layup. Then she heaved a 15-foot (4.6 m) shot that found the bottom of the net. Feaster capped her scoring outburst with a 3-point basket from the corner to put Harvard back in command, 69–65.

Harvard lost their next game in the tournament, but fans remember the team for taking down Stanford.

With less than a minute remaining in the game, Stanford threw a long pass down the court toward star player Olympia Scott. Feaster leaped in front of Scott to steal it away and seal the unlikely victory. Harvard's players swarmed the court as the final seconds ticked away. It remains the only time a 16-seed has ever beaten a 1-seed either in the men's or women's tournaments, and it stands as one of the greatest upsets in college basketball history.

NOT QUITE PERFECT

The 2007 New England Patriots seemed unstoppable. Tom Brady, that season's NFL Most Valuable Player (MVP), led the squad. The team had it all: a record-setting offense, a punishing defense, and the game's best head coach in Bill Belichick. After becoming the first team ever to finish the regular season 16–0, they cruised through the playoffs on their way to the Super Bowl.

Their opponent was the New York Giants, a team that had barely even made the playoffs at 10–6. It hardly seemed like a fair fight. For many fans and the media, the outcome of the game was never in doubt. The question wasn't whether the Patriots would win but rather how badly they would crush the overmatched Giants.

New York wasted no time reminding fans that the game still had to be played before the Patriots could be crowned as the greatest team in NFL history. New York took the opening kickoff and marched down the field on the longest-lasting drive in Super Bowl history—nine minutes and 59 seconds of game time—to score a field goal.

The Patriots' offense had set an NFL record for points that season, but the Giants held them at bay with a relentless pass rush. The first three quarters were a defensive slugfest, with the Patriots taking a 7–3 lead into the fourth quarter. What followed was 15 minutes of football that would leave fans breathless.

The Giants took the lead when quarterback Eli Manning rifled a touchdown pass to little-used receiver David Tyree. After the teams exchanged punts, Brady took over with just under eight minutes remaining in the game. The MVP was calm as he led the Patriots down the field. He connected with his favorite target, receiver Randy Moss, on a 6-yard touchdown pass to put New England back on top, 14–10.

THE GUARANTEE

Some athletes just can't resist predicting victory before a big event, and fans love the drama that such guarantees create. So when confident young New York Jets quarterback Joe Namath (*below*) guaranteed victory in Super Bowl III in 1969, people took notice.

Namath's claim might have been overlooked if it hadn't been so bold. The Jets represented the American Football League (AFL). The league had started in 1960 to compete with the NFL. By the late 1960s, the two groups had agreed to merge into one league, and the AFL and NFL's top teams met in the Super Bowl to decide a champion.

There was just one problem. The AFL had been crushed in each of the first two Super Bowls. There was little reason to believe that would change, even after Namath declared, "We're gonna win the game. I guarantee it." Fans and football experts expected Baltimore to win by more than two touchdowns.

Yet in one of the biggest upsets in Super Bowl history, the Jets beat the Colts, 16–7. The Jets smothered the Baltimore offense all game, forcing five Colts turnovers. Namath completed 17 passes to help his team make good on the most famous guarantee in sports history.

Then came a drive that many football fans will never forget. The Giants converted on a fourth-down play early in the drive. Later, near midfield on third down, Manning dropped back to pass. He barely had time to look down the field as New England defenders swarmed all around him. Manning, known as a slow-footed quarterback, somehow managed to sidestep the onslaught. As Patriots players tried to drag him down, Manning spun out of their grasp and heaved a pass down the field. Tyree leaped over his defender, grabbing the ball and pinning it against the top of his helmet. Somehow, he held on all the way to the ground for a jaw-dropping 32-yard completion.

A few plays later, Manning zipped a pass to receiver Plaxico Burress in the end zone. That gave the Giants the lead, 17–14. Brady came out for a few desperate throws down the field, but the New York defense held. The Giants swarmed the field, celebrating one of the biggest upsets in Super Bowl history.

Plaxico Burress catches a touchdown pass for New York, helping the Giants win the Super Bowl for the third time.

2 NEVER SAY DIE:

THE GREATEST COMEBACKS

Sometimes even when all hope seems lost, it isn't. One of the great lessons in sports is that quitting is never an option. No matter how dim the odds seem, a clutch performance can reverse a team's fortunes. Read on for some of the most incredible comebacks in sports history.

DOWN BUT NOT OUT

JANUARY 3, 1993

The halftime scoreboard said it all: Houston Oilers 28, Buffalo Bills 3. The Bills fans in Buffalo's Rich Stadium could hardly believe that their team seemed headed toward an embarrassing defeat against the Oilers in the playoffs.

Trailing by 25 points wasn't Buffalo's only problem. They were also short-handed. Star running back Thurman Thomas had left the game with a hip injury. Pro Bowl quarterback Jim Kelly was also out with an injury. The Buffalo offense was one of the league's most dangerous, but Thomas and Kelly were key players who made that offense go. Backup quarterback Frank Reich appeared overmatched in the first half and unable to step into Kelly's shoes.

Whatever dim hopes Buffalo fans were clinging to quickly disappeared early in the third quarter. Reich dropped back and fired a pass over the middle to tight end Keith McKeller, but McKeller couldn't haul it in. Instead, the ball bounced off his fingers and right into the arms of Houston defensive back Bubba McDowell. He was off to the races, dashing 58 yards for the touchdown. It was 35–3. The rout was on.

Without their team's two best offensive players, Buffalo fans had little hope. Frustrated people streamed toward the exits. A Houston radio announcer summed it up: "The lights are on here at Rich Stadium, but you might as well turn them off . . . this one is over."

Yet that's when something changed. Reich, who had been completely ineffective for more than half the game, suddenly started throwing pinpoint passes all around the field. Everything that had gone wrong for Buffalo earlier started going right.

Facing a 32-point deficit, the Bills marched down the field, scoring on a touchdown run from backup running back Kenneth Davis. Buffalo kicker Steve Christie then attempted an onside kick and recovered the ball himself. Four plays later, Reich fired a strike to wide receiver Don Beebe for a 38-yard touchdown. It was 35–17.

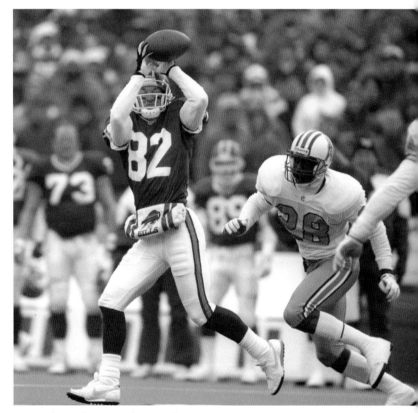

Don Beebe catches a pass from Frank Reich. Beebe caught three touchdown passes in 11 career playoff games with Buffalo.

Buffalo's defense also stepped up. On the next drive, they forced Houston to punt for the first time in the game. Reich quickly added another touchdown, this time on a pass to wide receiver Andre Reed.

After the kickoff, the Oilers wanted to keep the ball away from the Bills and run some time off the game clock to slow down Buffalo's momentum. But on the first play of Houston's drive, quarterback Warren Moon threw an interception to Henry Jones, who ran it back to Houston's 23-yard line. The Oilers defense stepped up on the next three plays, and the Bills faced 4th down and 5 yards to go from Houston's 18-yard line.

Buffalo head coach Marv Levy could have tried a field goal to cut the lead to eight points. But instead, he decided to go for the touchdown. Reich rewarded Levy's decision, rifling another touchdown pass to Reed. In less than seven minutes, the Bills had scored 28 points and cut the lead to four, 35–31.

In the fourth quarter, Moon led a drive down the field, ending at Buffalo's 14-yard line. The Oilers sent reliable kicker Al del Greco in for a field goal attempt. But holder Greg Montgomery fumbled the ball, and Buffalo recovered it.

Andre Reed was a Buffalo wide receiver for 15 seasons. He helped the team reach the Super Bowl four times, but the Bills lost all four games.

Reich and the Bills offense started yet another charge. With just over three minutes remaining on the game clock, Reich dropped back, scanned the field, and spotted Reed in the open. He fired a pass like a dart that Reed hauled in for the touchdown. It was 38–35, Buffalo.

It was a stunning comeback, but Houston wasn't done yet. Moon led the Oilers on a 63-yard drive in the closing minutes. The team lined up for a field goal, and this time, Montgomery held onto the ball. Del Greco made the kick to force overtime.

Houston won the coin toss to receive the ball first in overtime. On the third play of the drive, Moon tried to throw a pass to wide receiver Ernest Givens. But the ball sailed high. It flew over Givens and into the arms of Buffalo's Nate Odomes.

Buffalo, already deep in Houston territory, played it safe. They handed the ball to Davis two times. Then they sent Christie out to kick a field goal. He booted the 32-yard kick between the goalposts to win the game and finish off the biggest comeback in NFL history.

Buffalo's Nate Odomes runs with the ball after intercepting a Warren Moon pass in overtime. Moon threw four touchdown passes and two interceptions in the game.

he career of quarterback Frank Reich (*right*) was largely forgettable. Reich spent 13 seasons in the NFL, but he started just 20 regular-season games and had a record of 5–15. Yet when Reich led the Buffalo Bills to a 32-point playoff comeback over the Houston Oilers in 1993, it wasn't uncharted territory for him.

In college, Reich had performed a similar feat. He watched from the bench as the powerful Miami Hurricanes built a 31–0 halftime lead over his team, the Maryland Terrapins. Reich took the field in the second half, and he helped pull off what was, at the time, the biggest comeback in college football history. Maryland won the game, 42–40.

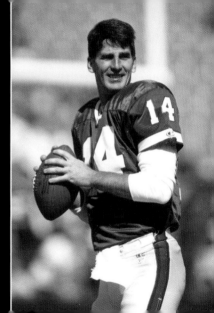

THE GREATEST COMEBACK THAT WASN'T
NOVEMBER 26, 1994

Football is king in Texas. Even high school games are big events. Some 20,000 people flocked to the 1994 state title game between Plano East and John Tyler, expecting a good battle. No one imagined that this would be one of the most amazing games ever played.

It didn't look like an epic clash for most of the game. John Tyler dominated play, building a 34–17 lead late in the fourth quarter. With 3:03 left on the game clock, John Tyler recovered a fumble and returned it for a touchdown. That made the score 41–17. The stadium began to empty as fans left an apparent blowout.

That's when the madness started. Plano East quarterback Jeff Whitley led a fast drive for a touchdown. The team recovered an onside kick and quickly scored another touchdown. Suddenly every bounce seemed to be going Plano East's way. They recovered another onside kick and scored. Another recovered onside kick and touchdown followed. John Tyler fans looked on in dismay as Whitley led Plano East to their fourth touchdown in less than three minutes to take a 44–41 lead.

It was about as improbable a comeback as the game of football has ever seen. Plano East fans celebrated, but the game wasn't over. The clock showed 24 seconds remaining in the fourth quarter—Plano East would have to kick off.

John Tyler's Roderick Dunn fielded the kickoff inside his own 5-yard line. Dunn charged up the field, cutting through Plano East players along the left sideline. Dunn ducked behind a wall of blockers as he raced down the field. No one could catch him. In a moment, the Plano East celebration turned into disbelief and heartache. Dunn crossed the goal line, and teammates mobbed him.

Just like that, it was over. One of the great comebacks in football history was erased. John Tyler won the state title, while Plano East saw the season slip through their fingers.

A DOZEN DOWN

Few fans were still paying attention
when Seattle Mariners outfielder
Al Martin grounded out in the
top of the fifth inning against the
Cleveland Indians. Seattle's Edgar
Martinez scored on the play, giving
the Mariners a 14–2 lead. Seattle, by
far baseball's best team in 2001 with a
record of 80–30, was in the middle of
a magical season. Cleveland appeared
to be just their latest victim.

Al Martin (*right*) and the Seattle Mariners ended the 2001
season with a record of 116–46. No team in Major League
Baseball history has won more than 116 games.

Seattle carried their 12-run
advantage into the bottom of the
seventh inning. By then even the most
hardened Cleveland fans had given up
on the game. The sold-out crowd at Cleveland's Jacobs Field had dwindled to a few
thousand souls.

Cleveland chipped away with three runs in the seventh. Then, in the eighth,
they added four more runs. It could have been more, but Kenny Lofton was thrown
out on a close call at home plate to end the inning.

After Seattle failed to score in the top of the ninth, Cleveland came to bat. They
still had a big hill to climb—the score was 14–9, and Seattle's relief pitchers had
been tough to hit all season. Eddie Taubensee reached first base on a single to start
the bottom of the ninth, but Seattle retired the next two batters. Cleveland, behind
by five runs, were down to their final out.

Marty Cordova kept the inning alive with a double. Seattle manager Lou Piniella had seen enough of his pitcher. He called to the bullpen, bringing in relief specialist Jeff Nelson, one of the best in the game.

Nelson walked the next batter to load the bases. Then catcher Einar Diaz lined a single to left field to score two runs. The score stood at 14–11.

Piniella pulled Nelson in favor of closer Kazuhiro Sasaki. But Seattle's implosion continued, and Sasaki allowed a single to Kenny Lofton to reload the bases.

Light-hitting shortstop Omar Vizquel stepped to the plate. Sasaki and Vizquel battled to a full count of three balls and two strikes. Then Vizquel drilled a line drive right down the first base line. Seattle first baseman Ed Sprague dove for the ball, but it was just out of reach. The remaining fans roared as three base runners raced home and Vizquel slid into third base. The comeback was complete. Seattle had surrendered its 12-run lead, and the game was headed to extra innings.

Two innings later, Cleveland capped off the most unlikely of wins when little-used infielder Jolbert Cabrera cracked a single with Lofton on second. Lofton, who was one of the fastest players in the game, raced around third base. Seattle outfielder Mark McLemore fielded the ball and fired it to home plate.

Kenny Lofton (*right*) scores the game-winning run for Cleveland. He scored more than 1,500 runs in his 17-year career.

But Lofton slid under the tag. The game was over, and the Indians celebrated as if they'd just won the World Series.

"It just proved that you never give up," recalled Cleveland slugger Jim Thome. "There's never a time in the game where you should give up and we proved it that night."

BREAKING THE CURSE
OCTOBER 2004

The Boston Red Sox were cursed. At least that's what many of the team's fans believed in 2004. The Red Sox had won the World Series in 1918. Three months later, Boston sold player Babe Ruth to their fiercest rival, the New York Yankees. Ruth became the game's biggest star, the Yankees became its greatest dynasty, and the Red Sox hadn't won a World Series since. The Curse of the Bambino was on.

The 2004 playoff clash between the two rivals appeared to be the latest expression of the curse. The Yankees were firmly in control, winning the first three games of the best-of-seven series. No team in baseball history had ever erased such a lead. In Game 4, New York was ahead by a run in the bottom of the ninth. They were an inning away from sweeping the Red Sox out of the playoffs and advancing to the World Series. An inning that would be pitched by the greatest closer the game has ever seen—Mariano Rivera.

The Red Sox seemed headed for defeat, but they were ready to go down swinging. Rivera walked the leadoff hitter, Kevin Millar. The speedy Dave Roberts came in to run for Millar. Roberts stole second base. That allowed him to score the tying run when Bill Mueller cracked a solid single. Boston's slim series hopes were alive. The game headed to extra innings.

The score remained tied in the bottom of the 12th inning. Boston slugger David Ortiz stepped to the plate with a runner on first base. Ortiz clubbed a pitch from

David Ortiz (*top*) celebrates with his teammates after helping Boston win Game 4. Many fans consider Ortiz the best designated hitter in baseball history.

New York's Paul Quantrill. The ball sailed deep into the right field seats. Boston had completed its incredible comeback to win, 6–4.

The series had appeared to be over, but it was just getting started. Ortiz was the hero again in Game 5, stroking a game-winning single in the 14th inning. Boston won Game 6 on the strength of a gutsy start from pitcher Curt Schilling, whose surgically repaired ankle bled through his sock during the game. Then they completed the unlikely comeback with a blowout victory in Game 7.

The Red Sox went on to win the 2004 World Series. The Curse of the Bambino had finally been broken.

VIRTUALLY IMPOSSIBLE
MARCH 20, 2016

Everything seemed to be going Northern Iowa's way in the early rounds of the 2016 NCAA Men's Basketball Tournament. A buzzer-beating 3-pointer had helped the

Panthers upset Texas in the final seconds of their first-round game. In the second round against the Texas A&M Aggies, the Panthers controlled the action. They had the ball with a 10-point lead and less than a minute to play in the game. The Aggies fouled guard Jeremy Morgan, who calmly sank two free throws to extend the Northern Iowa lead to 69–57.

The clock ticked down as Texas A&M brought the ball up the court. It dipped under 40 seconds as the Aggies heaved a 3-point shot that missed. It dwindled to 35 seconds when they grabbed the rebound and chucked up another missed shot. A 12-point lead with 35 seconds to play is all but impossible to overcome. One mathematical model put Northern Iowa's chances of winning the game at 99.99 percent.

A&M's Admon Gilder rose up and grabbed the ball as it clanged off the rim. Gilder quickly rose up and dropped the ball through the hoop. Northern Iowa took over with their lead cut to 10 points.

What followed was as improbable a comeback as college basketball has ever seen. Texas A&M put on heavy defensive pressure, and the Panthers had no idea how to counter it. Northern Iowa called a time-out and then lost the ball, leading to another A&M basket. With 23 seconds left in the fourth quarter, Jalen Jones stole the ball for the Aggies and slammed it home to cut the lead to six points.

Even that should have been too much to overcome. Northern Iowa had a 6-point lead and control of the ball with less than 25 seconds on the game clock. But on the next play, Northern Iowa's Wyatt Lohaus immediately passed the ball to no one, giving A&M the ball back without taking any time off the game clock. A few seconds later, Danuel House drained a 3-pointer. Just like that, the lead was down to three points, 69–66.

The Aggies set up their defense again. This time, Northern Iowa was ready. The Panthers threw a long pass to the streaking Klint Carlson. Carlson jammed it through the rim, and Northern Iowa fans breathed a sigh of relief. The lead was back to five points with just 18 seconds left in the quarter.

But Panthers fans didn't breathe easy for long. The Aggies rifled a pass down the court to Alex Caruso. Caruso weaved through the defense as he drove toward the hoop, and Northern Iowa fouled him as he made a basket. Caruso knocked down a free throw to make the score Northern Iowa 71, Texas A&M 69.

The offensive explosion by Texas A&M threw Northern Iowa into a panic. Senior point guard Wes Washpun received a pass with eight seconds on the clock. As soon as Washpun got the ball, the Aggies swarmed him. He threw the ball into the air—right into the hands of Texas A&M's Gilder, who drove to the basket and dropped it in.

Northern Iowa players (*in purple*) try to slow down Texas A&M in the game's final seconds.

Texas A&M had forced overtime, against all odds. The Aggies went on to win the game in double overtime. Northern Iowa's coaches and players were left wondering how they'd let a 12-point lead slip through their fingers in 35 seconds.

BRADY'S MASTERPIECE
FEBRUARY 5, 2017

The legacies of quarterback Tom Brady, head coach Bill Belichick, and the New England Patriots were secure long before Super Bowl LI on February 5, 2017. Since joining forces in 2000, Brady and Belichick had reached six Super Bowls, winning four of them. As Brady took the field against the Atlanta Falcons in 2017, he was in position to become the first quarterback in history to win five.

Atlanta had other ideas. The Falcons came out strong. They pressured Brady from the beginning, harassing and hitting the quarterback and forcing him into unusual errors. Meanwhile, Atlanta quarterback Matt Ryan was having his way with the New England defense. The Falcons rolled off score after score and appeared on their way to an easy victory.

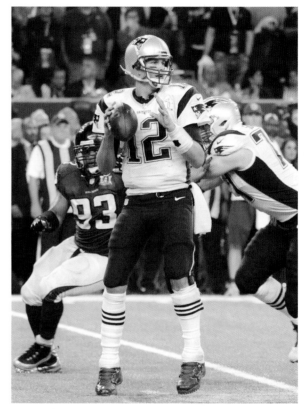

Tom Brady has thrown the most touchdown passes in NFL playoff history.

By late in the third quarter, the Falcons had a 28–3 lead. No team in Super Bowl history had ever come back from more than 10 points behind. The Falcons could have slowed down their play. They could have been content to run the ball and chew up the game clock. But they had reached the Super Bowl with a high-powered passing game, and they were unwilling to change in the biggest game of the year.

That strategy backfired, big time. Suddenly Ryan and the Atlanta offense began to stumble. Ryan fumbled the ball on a passing play. The Falcons struggled to get first downs. Brady, meanwhile, orchestrated one long scoring drive after another.

With just under six minutes to go in the fourth quarter, a touchdown pass from Brady to Danny Amendola cut the lead to eight points, 28–20. Atlanta's offense tried to respond. Wide receiver Julio Jones made an acrobatic diving catch at the New England 22-yard line. Atlanta kicker Matt Bryant had one of the most reliable legs in the game, and the team was well within his field goal range. Three more points probably would have put the game out of reach. But two plays later, New England sacked Ryan for a 12-yard loss. A 10-yard Falcons holding penalty followed, and Atlanta was forced to punt the ball to the Patriots.

Brady took over with 3:30 on the game clock. He led a drive that Patriots fans will never forget. Over 10 plays, New England relentlessly drove the ball down the field. Atlanta was helpless to stop them. Brady finished the drive with a touchdown pass to running back James White. Then White ran in the two-point conversion to tie the game. Falcons fans watched in disbelief as their team's 25-point lead disappeared.

James White (*bottom*) scored six touchdowns during the 2016–2017 playoffs, one more than he scored during the regular season.

The Patriots won the coin toss to start overtime and never looked back. Brady did it again, this time with an eight-play drive that ended with another White touchdown. It was over. The greatest comeback in Super Bowl history and one of the most incredible turnarounds in all of sports was complete.

THE MIRACLE OF BARCELONA
MARCH 8, 2017

By any reasonable measure, Football Club (FC) Barcelona was dead in the water in the 2017 Champions League quarterfinals. The tournament format called for a team to play two matches against the same opponent, using aggregate scoring to determine the winner. The team with the most combined goals over two games would advance.

It looked all but over after Paris Saint-Germain (PSG) dominated the first game, 4–0. But Barcelona came out on the attack on their home field in the second game, scoring two first-half goals. When Barcelona's Lionel Messi banged in a penalty kick early in the second half, the home fans began to feel that matching PSG in total goals was possible.

But in the 62nd minute, that optimism came crashing down. PSG's Edinson Cavani snuck in behind the Barcelona defense and buried a deflected ball in the back of the net. The goal was devastating for the home fans. It made the overall score 5–3 in favor of PSG. Because the rules awarded the tiebreaker to the team with more away goals (goals scored by the road team), Barcelona would need three goals to advance.

In the 88th minute, Neymar banged home a free kick for Barcelona to cut into the lead. It hardly seemed to matter since only two minutes of regulation time, plus a few minutes of injury time (time added to the clock because of play stoppages), remained. Barcelona still needed two goals, and PSG fans continued to celebrate.

Then, in injury time, the referee awarded Barcelona a penalty kick, which they converted into a goal. The overall score was 5–5, but Barcelona still needed a goal to win the tiebreaker.

In the 95th minute, with the match due to end at any moment, Barcelona sent their fans into a frenzy. The desperate team went into full-attack mode. Even goalkeeper Marc-Andre ter

Sergi Roberto scores Barcelona's sixth goal of the match.

Stegen ran down the field, leaving the Barcelona net empty. Neymar lobbed a high pass toward the PSG goal. Teammate Sergi Roberto managed to bring the pass in, whirl, and fire a shot that whizzed past the PSG goalkeeper. It was Barcelona's third goal in seven minutes, and it gave them the most improbable victory in Champions League history. The blue-shirted Barcelona players mobbed one another on the field as the stadium went wild.

"This is a crazy, unique sport," said Barcelona manager Luis Enrique. "No one stopped believing. The team [was] spectacular. We were rewarded in the end."

3 IMPLOSION:
THE MOST EPIC CHOKES

Clutch performances are the stuff of sporting legend but just as memorable are the times when athletes wilt under pressure. Then a team or athlete has victory in sight, but nerves, inability to execute, poor decision-making, or just plain bad luck leads to a crushing defeat. Choking is as compelling, in its own way, as the greatest clutch performances.

THROUGH THE LEGS
OCTOBER 25, 1986

In 1986 the Boston Red Sox were on the brink of finally breaking the Curse of the Bambino and winning the World Series for the first time since 1918. The Red Sox took a 3–2 series lead against the New York Mets into Game 6. The game went into extra innings, tied at 3–3. Boston scored two runs in the top of the 10th inning to take control, 5–3. They were just three outs away from a long-awaited championship.

Then 36-year-old Bill Buckner trotted out to first base for the bottom of the 10th inning. Buckner was playing on bad knees, and the Red Sox had replaced him in the late innings of several games earlier in the series, opting for a more capable defensive player.

However, Red Sox manager John McNamara didn't want to deprive the veteran of the chance to be on the field for the final out of the World Series, so he left Buckner in the game.

Boston relief pitcher Calvin Schiraldi retired the first two batters in the bottom of the 10th. The Red Sox were one out away from a championship.

The next two New York hitters got singles. Then Ray Knight, with two strikes against him, slapped a single of his own, driving in a run to make it 5–4. McNamara had seen enough. He pulled Schiraldi in favor of reliever Bob Stanley. Stanley promptly threw a wild pitch that allowed the tying run to score.

Everything was unraveling for Boston, but the team appeared to regain control when Stanley got Mookie Wilson to hit a weak ground ball to first base. Buckner needed only to field the ball and take a few steps to first base to send the game to the next inning. But he rushed the play, and the ball rolled between his legs. Knight dashed home, holding his helmet in disbelief, to score the winning run. Buckner looked on with his arms hanging at his sides as the Mets celebrated wildly.

The World Series went to Game 7, which the Mets won. Buckner had only played a small part of the collapse in Game 6, but he received most of the negative attention from fans and the media. His inability to field a routine ground ball still stands as one of the most epic chokes in sports history. It's a moment that haunts Red Sox fans to this day.

Bill Buckner played in more than 2,500 MLB games over 22 seasons, but fans will always remember him for one unfortunate moment.

MEMORY LAPSE

Chris Webber and the Michigan Wolverines were the talk of the college basketball world in 1992. Webber and four other Michigan freshmen were so good that fans called them the Fab Five. They advanced all the way to the NCAA Men's Basketball Tournament championship game before losing to Duke.

A year later, Webber and his teammates wanted to go one step farther. They once again tore through the NCAA Tournament and reached the championship game. This time, the North Carolina Tar Heels stood in their way.

It was a classic back-and-forth battle between two basketball powerhouses. North Carolina led in the closing minute. With 46 seconds to play, Michigan's Ray Jackson scored a basket to pull the Wolverines to within three points, 72–69. Michigan called their final time-out to set up their defense.

It worked. Michigan forced a North Carolina turnover. On the other end of the court, Webber scored a basket to trim North Carolina's lead to a single point.

Michigan quickly fouled North Carolina's Pat Sullivan to stop the clock. Sullivan made his first free throw but missed the second. Webber snagged the rebound with his team down by two points. The star forward looked around, searching for a teammate, but his fellow Wolverines were already running up the court. So Webber—not normally a ball handler—dribbled up the court himself.

The noise of the crowd was deafening. The game clock showed 20 seconds remaining in the fourth quarter. It was plenty of time for Michigan to set up a play. But Webber appeared to believe that he was running out of time. He rushed as North Carolina defenders collapsed around him, trapping him near the sideline.

Seeing the defense bearing down on him, Webber panicked. He stopped dribbling. His teammates were too far away to help, leaving him stranded.

That's when Webber made a huge mistake. He hugged the ball and formed the letter *T* with his hands. It was the signal for a time-out.

But Michigan had already used its final time-out. The referee blew the whistle and charged Michigan with a technical foul for calling a time-out that they didn't have. That meant North Carolina got two free throws and possession of the ball.

In an instant, Webber's lapse of memory had handed North Carolina the game. Shocked and visibly shaken, with tears streaming down his face, Webber could only watch as North Carolina celebrated the national championship. Few college basketball fans will ever forget the final play of Webber's college career.

Chris Webber (*right*) signals for a time-out his team doesn't have. He left Michigan after this game to begin a 15-year NBA career.

PULLING A VAN DE VELDE
JULY 18, 1999

French golfer Jean Van de Velde walked to the 18th and final hole of the 1999 British Open with a three-shot lead. He was just moments from claiming the British Open's trophy, the Claret Jug, and his first major golf title. The hole was a par 4, and with his big lead, Van de Velde could take as many as six strokes and still win the title. For a pro golfer, it should have been an easy task.

Van de Velde chose to take an aggressive opening shot with his most powerful club instead of a safer and more easily controlled shot. The strategy would have made sense if he'd needed to shoot par or better. But with a six-stroke cushion, a safe shot seemed like the obvious play. Yet Van de Velde lined up the tee shot and took a massive swing, sending his ball far off course and into long grass.

It was a mistake, but Van de Velde was still in good shape. All he had to do was recover on the next shot by safely shooting the ball back onto the middle of the course. Yet once again, Van de Velde tried for the big shot, hoping to reach the green. And again, his decision backfired horribly. The shot strayed to the right, dinged off a metal structure, and landed in knee-deep grass.

Van de Velde stands in the Barry Burn and considers his next move. The watery area is one of golf's most infamous obstacles.

Van de Velde was beginning to get flustered. He failed to make solid contact on his third shot, and the crowd gasped as he hit the ball into the Barry Burn, a watery area near the green. Van de Velde removed his shoes and socks, rolled up his pants, and waded into shin-deep water. He appeared to consider playing the ball as it lay—underwater—before sanity finally prevailed. Instead, he dropped the ball onto dry land, a move that came with a one-stroke penalty. Everyone at the course that day and the millions of fans following the action on TV watched in horror and confusion at one of the most puzzling meltdowns in golf history.

Remarkably, even after having done just about everything wrong on the 18th hole, Van de Velde still had a chance to win. But his fifth shot was also off the mark, this time finding its way into a sand trap. He reached the green on the sixth shot and finally sank the ball with his seventh shot. That forced a playoff, which he lost to Paul Lawrie.

Van de Velde never again came close to winning a major golf tournament. But his name lives on in infamy, as the phrase "pulling a Van de Velde" has come to describe any catastrophic sporting meltdown.

BARTMAN
OCTOBER 14, 2003

The Red Sox weren't the only team battling a so-called curse throughout most of the 20th century. Fans of the Chicago Cubs were convinced that their team was every bit as cursed. They hadn't won the World Series since 1908 and hadn't even appeared in it since 1945.

The 2003 Cubs were out to change that. Leading three games to two in the National League Championship Series and ahead 3–0 in Game 6, the Cubs were knocking on the door to the World Series. Then came a choke so big that even the team's fans got involved.

In the bottom of the eighth inning, lifelong Cubs fan Steve Bartman was enjoying the game from the front row along the left field line. With one out and a runner on second base, Luis Castillo of the Florida Marlins lofted a fly ball in foul territory. Left fielder Moises Alou tracked the ball to the wall. As Alou extended his arm to catch the ball, Bartman reached out. It deflected off Bartman's hands, preventing Alou from recording the out.

Had Alou caught the ball, the Cubs would have been just four outs from the World Series. Instead, the game unraveled for Chicago. Castillo ended up walking. What followed was a string of fielding miscues, wild pitches, and Marlins hits that resulted in eight runs. Florida went on to win the game and then the series.

Cubs fans were furious with

Steve Bartman (*in blue hat with arms outstretched*) deflects the ball in the eighth inning. He received death threats and went into hiding after the game.

Bartman. His actions certainly hurt the team he loved, but they were far from the only reason the Cubs lost. He played a small but memorable part in one of the most painful chokes in baseball history.

WIDE RIGHT

The New Orleans Saints almost pulled off a miracle in their 2003 NFL game against the Jacksonville Jaguars. The Saints had the ball on their own 25-yard line with seven seconds remaining in the game. They trailed Jacksonville 20–13. New Orleans needed a touchdown to force overtime and keep their playoff hopes alive.

Quarterback Aaron Brooks took the snap and fired a pass to wide receiver Donte Stallworth at midfield. Stallworth turned and charged, eluding tacklers as the clock ticked down to zero. With defenders crashing in on Stallworth, he pitched the ball backward to teammate Michael Lewis, who charged forward to

Jerome Pathon scores to give the Saints a chance to tie the game.

Jacksonville's 25-yard line. Lewis pitched it to Deuce McAllister, who in turn threw it backward to Jerome Pathon. Pathon turned and sprinted, using a block from Brooks to dive into the end zone.

It was an unbelievable turn of events. Officials delayed the game for several minutes as they looked at video of the play to make sure it had been legal. They decided the touchdown was good. In one of the most amazing last-second plays in NFL history, the Saints had seemingly saved their season.

All that remained to tie the game was the extra point, a 17-yard kick that NFL kickers made about 99 percent of the time. Kicker John Carney trotted onto the field. The snap was good, and the hold was clean. But the ball darted hard to the right when it came off Carney's foot. It sailed wide of the goalpost—no good! The Saints playoff hopes were dead, and Carney—an otherwise reliable kicker—would live in infamy for his embarrassing choke.

SHOWBOATING TO SILVER
FEBRUARY 17, 2006

Snowboarders don't get a lot of chances to become international celebrities. Yet as the 2006 Winter Olympics approached, that's exactly what US star Lindsey Jacobellis was becoming. Her talent and fun-loving style had made her a household name. Her sport, snowboard cross, featured four racers in a breakneck charge down a mountain. It was one part snowboarding and one part NASCAR.

Jacobellis was a heavy favorite for the gold medal, and she showed why in the final race. She sliced her way down the slope, sailing over jumps and cutting perfectly through turns as she pulled ahead of the other racers. She came out of the final turn with an untouchable lead, needing to clear just two simple jumps to claim Olympic gold.

The 20-year-old looked back over her shoulder and saw that the closest competitor was far behind her. As she launched over the first jump and sailed through the air, she decided to do a little trick to celebrate her pending victory. Jacobellis reached down and grabbed her board, a trick called a backside method grab.

The grab is a basic move that she expected to land easily. But something went horribly wrong. Jacobellis landed awkwardly, with her board coming down on an edge. She couldn't recover and went toppling over as the crowd gasped in disbelief. Jacobellis quickly bounced up and tried to regain speed over the final small jump,

Lindsey Jacobellis slides on her back before recovering to finish second. She went on to compete in the 2010, 2014, and 2018 Olympic Games.

but it was too late. Switzerland's Tanja Frieden streaked by to win the race just before Jacobellis reached the finish line in second place. The US racer could only watch in disbelief as Frieden celebrated.

Jacobellis remains one of the most successful snowboarders in history. Yet for many, the enduring memory of her career will be that fateful backside method grab and how it cost her a gold medal.

4 THE FINAL SECONDS:

MEMORABLE CLUTCH PERFORMANCES

For sports fans, nothing beats those moments when an athlete does something incredible with the game on the line. Buzzer-beaters, walk-off home runs, and overtime touchdown passes are drama-filled plays that keep us coming back for more. Read on to relive a few of the most memorable clutch plays in the history of sports.

FLUTIE MAGIC
NOVEMBER 23, 1984

The Orange Bowl in Miami, Florida, was buzzing. The Miami Hurricanes, the top-ranked team in college football, had just scored a touchdown to take a 45–41 lead over the Boston College (BC) Eagles. The clock showed just 28 seconds remaining in the game.

Few had expected the Eagles to keep the score close. BC had played the nation's best team down to the wire. But behind by four points with less than 30 seconds on the clock, even some of BC's players later admitted that they thought the game was over.

Not Eagles quarterback Doug Flutie. The undersized leader of the underdog team wasn't ready to concede. After a holding penalty against Miami on the drive's first play, only 20 seconds remained. On the next play, Flutie scrambled and found a receiver who was tackled at the Miami 48-yard line. After an incomplete pass, only six seconds remained—time for just one more play.

The Hurricanes knew what was coming. Flutie had to throw a deep pass to the end zone. He held the ball and waited as his receivers streaked down the field. A Miami defender broke through Boston College's blockers, but Flutie slipped away, keeping his gaze down the field. The final seconds ticked off the clock. By the time he was ready to throw, Flutie had backed up all the way to Boston College's 37-yard line. He hurled the ball with all his strength.

The ball sailed in a long, high arc. As it approached the end zone, two Miami defenders collided as they tried to knock it down. That gave BC's Gerard Phelan an opening. With his feet in the end zone, Phelan caught the ball against his chest. He clung to it as he fell to the ground. The referee made the signal: touchdown!

The Orange Bowl fell into a stunned silence. More than 60 yards away, Flutie still didn't know what had happened—he couldn't see over the taller players in front of him. He barely believed it when he finally saw the touchdown signal. The celebration was on, and Flutie's magical Hail Mary remains one of the most memorable passes in college football history.

Some fans thought Doug Flutie (*top*) was too short to play quarterback, but after succeeding in college, he played in the NFL and the Canadian Football League.

GIBSON'S BLAST

OCTOBER 15, 1988

The Los Angeles Dodgers faced a bleak situation at home in Game 1 of the 1988 World Series. They trailed the Oakland A's 4–3 in the bottom of the ninth inning. That meant Oakland's dominant closer, Dennis Eckersley, was on the pitcher's mound. He had been close to unhittable all year. He quickly retired the first two batters he faced.

STRIKE UP THE BAND

One of the most memorable finishes in sports history came in a college football game between California and Stanford in 1982. Stanford, the home team, booted a field goal with just four seconds left on the game clock to take a 20–19 lead.

On the kickoff, Cal executed a series of lateral passes (passes that do not travel forward) to cut through the Stanford tacklers. As the play continued, the Stanford band, thinking that the game was over, marched onto the far end of the field to get the celebration started.

Cal's Mariet Ford carried the ball with a group of teammates toward the end zone—right into the midst of more than 100 band members. Surrounded by the band, Ford made a lateral pass to Kevin Moen, who charged through a thick mass of band members and into the end zone for the winning score. In the end zone, Moen slammed into a trombone player, putting a unique exclamation point on one of the wildest finishes in sports history.

The Dodgers were down to their final out. Manager Tommy Lasorda decided to pinch hit and sent Mike Davis to the plate. He also sent light-hitting Dave Anderson to the on-deck circle. The A's, seeing that Anderson would be up next, chose to pitch to Davis very carefully. They knew Davis was a powerful hitter, and they'd rather take their chances with Anderson.

Davis drew a walk. Lasorda quickly made his next move. He'd never intended to let Anderson hit. He had one other option—slugger Kirk Gibson.

Gibson was one of the game's best hitters. But injuries to both of his legs—his left hamstring and his right knee—had forced him to the bench for the series opener. The superstar hobbled to the plate as the LA crowd roared.

It was a huge gamble. Gibson wasn't a speedster even under the best conditions. With two bad legs, he could barely run. If he hit anything on the ground, he'd be thrown out easily and the game would be over.

It appeared Lasorda's tactic would backfire. Like many hitters that season, Gibson looked overmatched against Eckersley, flailing wildly. But the seasoned hitter worked the pitcher into a full count.

Eckersley delivered the pitch. Gibson was ready for it, taking a mighty hack. Without the full use of his legs, it was a strange-looking, off-balance swing, but Gibson made it work. The ball jumped off his bat and soared into the right field seats. Home run! The crowd went wild as Gibson limped around the bases, pumping his fist in celebration. Gibson's amazing home run remains one of the iconic moments in World Series history, and it sparked the Dodgers to a championship.

Dodgers fans will never forget Kirk Gibson's joyful trip around the bases after his World Series home run.

MR. OCTOBER

Few players in sports history are more celebrated by fans for clutch performances than outfielder Reggie Jackson (*right*). The Hall of Famer was one of baseball's top power hitters in the 1970s and early 1980s, and he earned the nickname Mr. October for his World Series heroics. Jackson played in five World Series with the A's and the Yankees. In 27 games, he belted 10 home runs with a .357 batting average. His crowning achievement came in the final game of the 1977 series. Jackson hit home runs in three consecutive at bats to help clinch the series for the Yankees.

THE SHOT
MARCH 28, 1992

No moment in college basketball history is more iconic than the final shot of the 1992 NCAA Men's Basketball Tournament game featuring Kentucky and Duke. The two basketball powerhouses battled it out in a thrilling back-and-forth overtime battle that came down to the final moments.

In the closing seconds of overtime, Kentucky's Sean Woods drove toward the basket and threw up a running one-handed shot to give Kentucky a 103–102 lead. Just 2.1 seconds remained on the game clock, and Duke had to go the length of the court to score.

Duke forward Grant Hill took the ball. No Kentucky player guarded

Christian Laettner played 13 seasons in the NBA, but basketball fans remember him best for his game-winning shot against Kentucky.

Hill, leaving him a clear view of the court. He heaved the ball toward star forward Christian Laettner, who battled for position near the opposite free-throw line.

Laettner leaped into the air, hauling in the long pass with one hand. The clock started ticking as soon as he touched it. Kentucky defenders rushed toward him. Most players would have hurried their shot, knowing time was about to expire. But Laettner knew exactly how much he could do in two seconds. "I remember thinking 2.1 seconds felt more like 20 seconds," said sportswriter Rick Bozich.

Laettner dribbled once, faking a move to his right. Then he pivoted left and launched a jump shot. Just 0.3 seconds remained on the game clock as the ball left his hands. It sailed through the air. *SWISH!* The crowd erupted as Laettner raised his arms in victory. Duke player Thomas Hill held his head in disbelief. Hill and everyone watching the game knew that they had just seen one of the most clutch moments in sports history.

THE FLU GAME
JUNE 11, 1997

Michael Jordan should not have been on the court for Game 5 of the 1997 NBA Finals against the Utah Jazz. Jordan, widely regarded as the greatest basketball player in NBA history, was sick with the flu—or possibly food poisoning. Unable to keep anything down before the game, Jordan was suffering from dehydration and exhaustion.

It showed early in the game. The Chicago Bulls superstar appeared sluggish. He wasn't his dominant self. Utah took advantage of it, building an 8-point lead after three quarters.

That's when Jordan turned it on. He scored baskets in bunches. He grabbed rebounds and dished out assists. And every time he got a break, he collapsed onto the bench.

Michael Jordan during Game 5 of the 1997 NBA Finals. He won six NBA championships and scored the fourth most career points in league history.

The game was tied, 85–85, in the final minute of the fourth quarter. Jordan passed the ball to teammate Scottie Pippen. As Pippen looked for a shot, Utah's defense rushed him. Pippen quickly zipped the ball back out to Jordan, beyond the 3-point line. Jordan rose up and launched a shot that sailed through the air and into the net. The Bulls were ahead and kept their lead. Jordan scored 38 points in the game.

As the final horn sounded, he appeared close to collapsing. He leaned on Pippen, appearing to need help just to walk off the floor. Two days later, Jordan scored 39 points to help finish off the Jazz and deliver a fifth NBA championship to Chicago fans.

Jordan had long ago cemented his legacy as one of sports' all-time clutch athletes. But his performance in the flu game proved nothing could keep him down and only built on his legend.

CHASTAIN'S GOLDEN GOAL
JULY 10, 1999

The Women's World Cup was just eight years old in 1999. Despite soccer's status as the most popular sport in the world, the women's game was still struggling to gain a following. One clutch goal helped to change that.

The host nation, the United States, faced China in the title game. For 120 minutes, the two teams engaged in a defensive battle, with neither team able to put the ball in the net. The game came down to penalty kicks. Each team would get five tries.

The teams were tied 4–4 in the final round of penalty kicks. Defender Brandi Chastain could clinch the Women's World Cup for the United States with a goal. Chastain, who had missed a penalty kick against China three months earlier, stood before the ball. Unlike most players who have a preferred kicking foot, Chastain could kick just as well with either one. That left Chinese goalkeeper Gao Hong guessing which foot Chastain would use. Chastain quickly approached the ball and booted it with her left foot toward the right corner of the goal. The goalkeeper dove for it, but the ball slid past her outstretched fingers.

Goal! US fans roared as Chastain ripped off her jersey and fell to her knees. Her teammates rushed together to celebrate. Chastain's clutch goal helped spark a new level of interest in women's soccer, and it helped to launch a US dynasty in the sport.

Brandi Chastain's goal celebration became an iconic image for US soccer fans.

THE PUTT
JUNE 15, 2008

Few athletes have defined clutch as Tiger Woods did in his best years. Woods always seemed to hit his best shots at the biggest moments, and that's exactly what he did at the 2008 US Open.

Woods came to the 18th hole at Torrey Pines Golf Course trailing Rocco Mediate by a single stroke. Just being that close was quite an accomplishment. Woods was less than two months removed from knee surgery. His other leg was also injured. He had played little in the weeks before the tournament. For four days, Woods hobbled across the long, sweeping course in La Jolla, California. He was in a lot of pain, grunting and groaning with nearly every shot.

Yet despite his injuries, Woods was in position to win the tournament as he teed off on the 18th hole, a long par 5. It didn't start well. Woods hit his tee shot into a sand trap. He slammed his club against the ground after his second shot landed in the tall grass. But his third shot was a beauty. Woods dropped the ball onto the green, 15 feet (4.6 m) from the hole.

Woods, wearing a bright red shirt as he always did on the final day of a tournament, stood over the ball as the crowd fell silent. It was a long putt, and Woods needed to make it to force a playoff. He leaned forward, eyed the hole, and then hit his shot. The ball made a beeline for the hole, catching the right edge and dropping in. Woods screamed in celebration as the crowd went wild.

Woods had done it. With two bad legs, he had tied Mediate. Woods finished the job the following day when he beat Mediate in the playoff to claim his 14th—and to date, his final—major championship.

BY A FINGERTIP
AUGUST 16, 2008

US swimmer Michael Phelps was the talk of the 2008 Summer Olympics. Phelps dominated the men's swimming events, winning many of his races by huge margins. He racked up six gold medals and was on the hunt for number seven in the 100-meter butterfly.

Tiger Woods celebrates at the US Open. He was on pace to become the most successful golfer in history before injuries interrupted his career.

This one wouldn't be so easy. Serbian swimmer Milorad Cavic dove into the pool with a perfect start. He quickly pulled ahead of the field.

Phelps got closer on the turn, when swimmers launch themselves off the far wall and head back the other way. But Cavic still held a comfortable lead.

As the swimmers approached the near wall and the end of the race, Cavic still led. Phelps was closing in, but he appeared to be running out of time. As Cavic neared the wall, he stretched out his hand, reaching for victory. While Cavic stretched, Phelps never stopped swimming. He took one final stroke.

It was just enough. Phelps' fingertip touched the wall a fraction of a second before Cavic's. But the finish was too close for the swimmers to tell who had won. After a

Phelps (*right*) beats Cavic to the wall. The US swimmer won the race by 0.01 of a second.

few agonizing seconds, the scoreboard flashed the final result. Phelps had done it. It was his seventh gold medal at the 2008 Olympics and another huge victory for the swimmer who would become the most decorated athlete in Olympic Games history.

FREESE FRAME
OCTOBER 27, 2011

The St. Louis Cardinals were the comeback kids in 2011. On August 24, they had trailed the Atlanta Braves by 10.5 games in the standings. Coming back from so far behind with just over a month to play in the season was a nearly impossible task, but they pulled it off and clinched a playoff spot on the final day.

The Cardinals rode that momentum all the way to the World Series against the Texas Rangers. Once again, the Cardinals were backed into a corner. Texas led the series, 3–2.

In Game 6, Texas closer Neftali Feliz was on the mound for the ninth inning. The Rangers led, 7–5. The Cardinals had runners on first and second, but there were two outs. Feliz threw two quick strikes to St. Louis third baseman David Freese. The Cardinals were down to their final strike.

Feliz looked in at the catcher and delivered the pitch. Freese was ready. He lined the ball over the glove of a leaping defender, and he was off to the races. Both base runners scored, and Freese slid into third base with a triple. The St. Louis crowd roared as their team tied the game.

Their joy was short-lived, however. Texas bounced back in the top of the 10th inning with a two-run Josh Hamilton home run. The Rangers were back on top, 9–7.

St. Louis was on the edge of defeat yet again. With two out and two runners on base in the bottom of the 10th, Cardinals outfielder Lance Berkman was down to his final strike. But as usual, the Cardinals refused to die, and Berkman stroked a single to center field. Both runners scored to tie the game once more.

The Rangers failed to score in the top of the 11th. Freese led off the bottom half of the inning. The pitch count stood at three balls and two strikes. Texas relief pitcher Mark Lowe delivered a changeup—a pitch designed to throw off a hitter's timing by traveling more slowly than a fastball. It didn't fool Freese. The crowd went wild as he blasted the ball 429 feet (131 m) over the center field wall— his second clutch hit of the game. The Cardinals won Game 7 the next day, and Freese won the World Series MVP award.

David Freese watches the ball sail into the outfield before racing around the bases for a triple in the ninth inning. The World Series win was the 11th championship for the Cardinals, the second most in baseball history.

MINNEAPOLIS MIRACLE
JANUARY 14, 2018

The Minnesota Vikings were on the edge of disaster. US Bank Stadium in Minneapolis had been filled with thunderous cheers for most of the January 14, 2018, playoff game against the New Orleans Saints. But as the game clock ticked away in the fourth quarter, the crowd was almost silent.

Vikings fans had roared as their team took a 17–0 lead early in the game, but New Orleans quarterback Drew Brees engineered a thrilling second-half comeback. With just 25 seconds to play in the game, the Saints kicked a field goal to take a 24–23 advantage.

The Vikings had the ball on their own 39-yard line with 10 seconds on the clock. They needed to gain about 20 yards to attempt a long field goal, but with no time-outs remaining, it was doubtful they would even have time to line up for the kick. Case Keenum, who had started the season as the team's backup quarterback, took the snap. Vikings receivers streaked down the sidelines. They hoped to catch a long pass and then quickly step out of bounds to stop the clock.

With defenders all around him, Keenum heaved the ball down the field. Wide receiver Stefon Diggs rose up and snagged the pass. As Diggs came down with the ball just inches from the sideline, New Orleans defender Marcus Williams dove to make the tackle. Williams wanted to tackle Diggs in bounds, keeping the clock running and ending the game. Instead, Williams missed and crashed into another Saints defender. Diggs spun and put one hand down on the field to balance himself. When he looked up, he saw nothing but open space in front of

him. As Vikings fans erupted in a deafening cheer, Diggs streaked down the field. He crossed the goal line as the clock struck 0:00. Touchdown!

The Vikings won the game and shocked the sports world. It was the first time in NFL playoff history that a winning touchdown in regulation time had been the last play in a game. And it was a moment that Vikings and Saints fans will never forget.

Stefon Diggs catches the ball as defender Marcus Williams (*center*) goes for the tackle.

5 CLUTCH:

THE SCIENCE AND PSYCHOLOGY OF THE BIG MOMENT

While most fans love the idea of a clutch performance, it's hard to pin down exactly what qualities make a player or a team clutch. Many people agree that certain players excel under pressure. Yet many sports analysts say that there are no consistently clutch players and that stats agree.

THE SCIENCE OF CLUTCH

Everyone from coaches and players to psychologists have tried to define just what it takes to be clutch. Not everyone agrees, but there are some basic ideas. One theory suggests that clutch performances come from a combination of elements, including brain chemistry and the ability to focus.

Chemicals, such as hormones, in the human body help it to do its job. Scientists who study the idea of clutch performance often focus on one hormone, called adrenaline. The body releases adrenaline in stressful situations. The chemical heightens one's awareness and prepares the body for action in the face of danger, a reaction commonly called the fight-or-flight response. Athletes who perform well in high-pressure situations are able to handle this adrenaline rush and turn it into positive performances.

An ability called hyperfocus may be a second key element. This is the brain's ability to focus entirely on a single task. People who lack this ability may not be able to channel all of their mental resources in high-pressure situations. They may be distracted by the situation or plagued with doubt. People with hyperfocus are able to set the pressure aside and concentrate only on performing to the best of their abilities.

A SKEPTICAL VIEWPOINT

Not everyone agrees that clutch performers even exist. We may consider athletes who have performed well in pressure situations to be clutch, but those performances may be nothing more than random chance. According to sportswriter and former Toronto Blue Jays executive Keith Law, "There is such a thing as clutch hits, but not [consistently] clutch hitters. If you look at the numbers and try to find that hitter, you'll find that he doesn't exist."

Some believe that it's impossible to gain new abilities in a pressure-packed situation. They insist that one cannot become a better passer, shooter, or hitter just because the game is on the line.

Baseball legend Reggie Jackson dismisses this argument. "Are you telling me that when you're down to one shot, Michael Jordan is no different from anybody else?" Jackson argued. "How can you tell me Tiger Woods doesn't play better under pressure? [Golf legend] Jack Nicklaus was the same as anybody else? I'm not buying it."

Michael Jordan came up clutch many times during his 15-year NBA career.

Of course, Jordan, Woods, and Nicklaus were the best players in their sports during their prime playing years. Did they perform well in pressure situations because they were clutch? Or did they just come up big when it counted because they were the best in any situation—high pressure or otherwise?

MENTAL PREPARATION

Regardless of the arguments against clutch ability being a measurable trait, most players believe that it's a real thing, and many train themselves to be clutch. Sports psychologists help athletes achieve the right mindset to succeed. Many players use techniques such as imagining themselves succeeding in clutch situations to prepare for success in real life. Others use calming techniques to quiet the mind and treat clutch situations just like any other moment.

Psychologist Tim Woodman says that a person's range of performance varies with pressure. He says that in low-pressure situations, an athlete's performance is more predictable, without major swings for the good or the bad. However, that changes when a person feels stress. "If you put [athletes]

US gymnast Simone Biles competes in the floor exercise during the 2016 Olympic Games. She won four gold medals in 2016.

in a very high-worry situation, like Olympic Games, what you find is that their best performance is significantly better than before and their worst performance is significantly worse," Woodman says. "So what that tells you is that when you're under a very high-stress situation, you either perform very well or very badly."

Do clutch performers really exist? And if so, what makes them different from the choker or the average performer? Is it the way the brains of top athletes are wired? Is it mental toughness? Training and preparation? Or is it something harder to identify?

For most fans, science and statistics simply can't define what makes a clutch performance so compelling. From epic performances to crushing collapses, the most pressure-packed moments are what keep sports fans coming back for more.

SOURCE NOTES

8 Fred Van Ness, "A Horse Named Upset Beats Man o' War," *New York Times*, August 13, 1919, http://www.nytimes.com/packages/html/sports/year_in_sports/08.13.html.

11 Steven Marcus, "'Do You Believe in Miracles? YES!' . . . We Did During USA Hockey Team's Run to Gold Medal," *Newsday*, last modified February 22, 2015, https://www.newsday.com/sports/hockey/do-you-believe-in-miracles-yes-we-did-during-usa-hockey-team-s-run-to-gold-medal-1.9963102.

12 Associated Press, "No. 16 Harvard over No. 1 Stanford Still Resonates 10 Years Later," *ESPN*, last modified March 18, 2008, http://www.espn.com/espn/wire/_/section/ncw/id/3300407.

14 Les Carpenter, "Nothing like Namath's Guarantee," *Washington Post*, January 30, 2007, http://www.washingtonpost.com/wp-dyn/content/article/2007/01/29/AR2007012901789.html.

17 "Greatest Games—1993 AFC Wild Card Game: Bills 41, Oilers 38 OT," Bills Zone, October 3, 2003, https://web.archive.org/web/20070608090426/http://www.billszone.com/mtlog/archives/2003/10/03/greatest_games_1993_afc_wild_card_gamebills_41_oilers_38_ot.php.

24 Zack Meisel, "A Comeback for the Ages: An Oral History of the Cleveland Indians' Historic Rally against the Seattle Mariners 15 Years Ago," *Cleveland.com*, August 5, 2016, http://www.cleveland.com/tribe/index.ssf/2016/08/cleveland_indians_seattle_mari_39.html.

31 John Sinnott, "Champions League 2017: Barcelona Routs Paris Saint-Germain 6–1 in Astonishing Comeback," *CNN*, March 9, 2017, http://edition.cnn.com/2017/03/08/football/barcelona-paris-saint-germain-champions-league/index.html.

47 Dana O'Neil, "From Hill to Laettner, 25 Years Later," *ESPN*, March 21, 2017, http://www.espn.com/espn/feature/story/_/id/18905808/remembering-christian-laettner-epic-ncaa-tournament-buzzer-beater-25-years-later.

57 Tom Verducci, "Does Clutch Hitting Truly Exist? Not in the Stats Community, but Don't Try Telling That to the Guys on the Field," *Sports Illustrated*, April 5, 2014, https://www.si.com/vault/2004/04/05/8210148/does-clutch-hitting-truly-exist-not-in-the-stats-communitybut-dont-try-telling-that-to-the-guys-on-the-field.

57 Ibid.

58–59 Jeff Wise, "The Science of Sports: Is There Such a Thing as a Clutch Performer?," *Psychology Today*, June 9, 2010, https://www.psychologytoday.com/blog/extreme-fear/201006/the-science-sports-is-there-such-thing-clutch-performer.

GLOSSARY

closer: a relief pitcher whose role is to get the last few outs of a baseball game when his team is ahead

dehydration: a lack of water in the body

dynasty: a long period of dominance by one athlete or team

favorite: a team or athlete that is expected to win

guard: a basketball player usually responsible for handling the ball and shooting

hyperfocus: the ability to focus intensely on a single task

major championship: one of the four biggest golf tournaments of the year: the Masters, the British Open, the US Open, and the PGA Championship

onside kick: a short kick that can be recovered by either football team

par: the standard score for each hole on a golf course

thoroughbred: a horse breed known for its racing ability

underdog: a team or athlete expected to lose a game

upset: a game in which an underdog player or team beats a favorite

FURTHER READING

Books

Bryant, Howard. *Legends: The Best Players, Games, and Teams in Basketball*. New York: Philomel Books, 2017.

Doeden, Matt. *The Super Bowl: Chasing Football Immortality*. Minneapolis: Millbrook Press, 2017.

———. *The World Series: Baseball's Biggest Stage*. Minneapolis: Millbrook Press, 2014.

Gifford, Clive. *Champions League Fact File*. London: Carlton Books, 2017.

Jacobs, Greg. *The Everything Kids' Football Book: All-Time Greats, Legendary Teams, and Today's Favorite Players—with Tips on Playing Like a Pro*. Avon, MA: Adams Media, 2016.

Mattern, Joanne. *Legendary Athletic Achievements*. Mankato, MN: 12-Story Library, 2018.

Websites

MLB Kids
http://mlb.mlb.com/mlb/kids/index.jsp

NFL Rush
http://www.nflrush.com

100 Greatest Moments in Sports History
https://www.si.com/100-greatest

Sports Illustrated Kids
https://www.sikids.com

What Makes an Athlete Clutch?
https://blogs.psychcentral.com/sports-couch/2014/06/what-makes-an-athlete-clutch

INDEX

ABOUT THE AUTHOR

Matt Doeden began his career as a sportswriter, covering everything from high school sports to the NFL. Since then he has written hundreds of children's and young adult books on topics ranging from history to sports to current events. Many of his titles were Junior Library Guild selections. His book *Darkness Everywhere: The Assassination of Mohandas Gandhi* was listed among the Best Children's Books of the Year by the Children's Book Committee at Bank Street College. Doeden lives in Minnesota with his wife and two children.

PHOTO ACKNOWLEDGMENTS

The images in this book are used with the permission of: Michael Appleton/NY Daily News Archive/Getty Images, p. 4; Bettmann/Getty Images, p. 6; AP Photo, p. 8; Steve Powell/Getty Images, p. 10; AP Photo/Aaron Suozzi, p. 12; Focus on Sport/Getty Images, pp. 14, 28, 33, 45, 46; Jim Davis/The Boston Globe/Getty Images, p. 15; Rick Stewart/Getty Images, pp. 17, 19; Joel Zwink/Getty Images, p. 18; Mitchell Layton/Getty Images, p. 20; RON KUNTZ/REUTERS/Newscom, p. 22; DAVID MAXWELL/AFP/Getty Images, p. 23; Ezra Shaw/Getty Images, p. 25; Shane Bevel/NCAA Photos/Getty Images, p. 27; Elsa/Getty Images, p. 29; Albert Llop/Anadolu Agency/Getty Images, p. 31; David E. Klutho/Sports Illustrated/Getty Images, p. 35; PA Images/Alamy Stock Photo, p. 36; Allen Fredrickson/REUTERS/Newscom, p. 38; Al Messerschmidt/Getty Images, p. 39; LORENVU/DPPI-SIPA/Icon SMI 547/Newscom, p. 41; Boston College/Collegiate Images/Getty Images, p. 43; Damian Strohmeyer/Sports Illustrated/Getty Images, p. 47; Brian Bahr/Getty Images, p. 48; ROBERTO SCHMIDT/AFP/Getty Images, p. 50; ROBYN BECK/AFP/Getty Images, p. 51; Nick Laham/Getty Images, p. 52; Rob Carr/Getty Images, p. 54; Hannah Foslien/Getty Images, p. 55; JEFF HAYNES/AFP/Getty Images, p. 57; Mark Reis/Colorado Springs Gazette/TNS/Getty Images, p. 58. Design elements: Vaskina mat/Shutterstock.com; Vector Tradition SM/Shutterstock.com; gigello/Shutterstock.com.

Front cover: Ronald Martinez/Getty Images. Flap: Hannah Foslien/Getty Images.

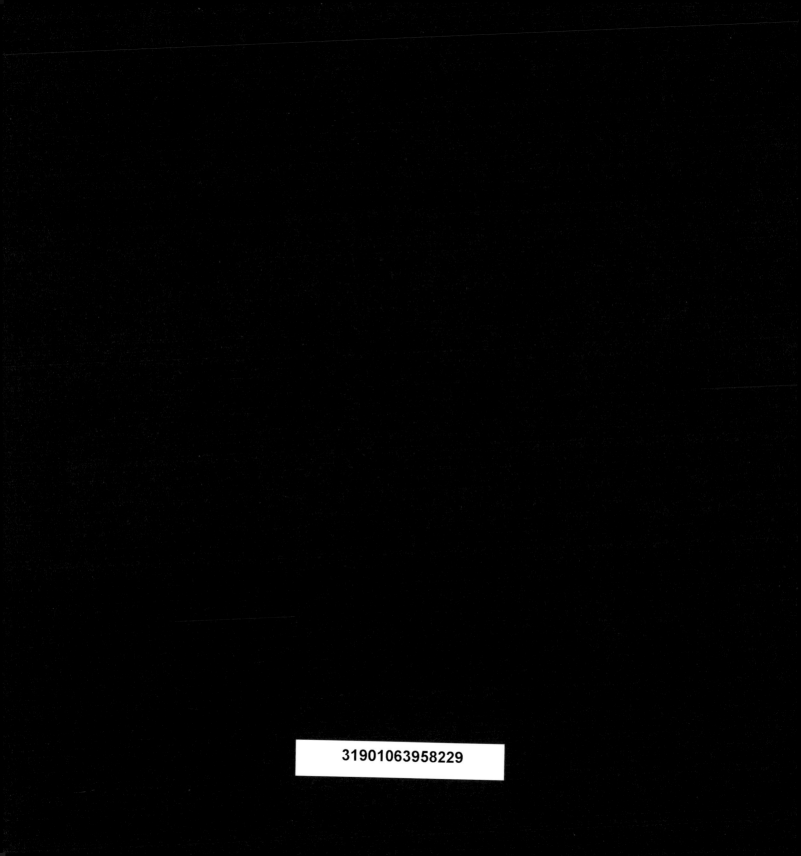

31901063958229